Cover and interior photography: Steve Speer
Photograph of Steve Speer: Todd Korol
Cover and interior design: Acorn Communications Inc.
Duotone image prep: Steve Speer
Managing Editor: Lia Robinson, BOMA Calgary
Project Manager: Jay de Nance, Fairfield Commercial Real Estate

With special thanks to Michael L. Kehoe, Fairfield Commercial Real Estate

Type faces used in this publication: Trajan Pro and Optima *(plate titles)*,
ITC Galliard *(section heads and body copy)*,
Caslon 540 *(main title)*.
Paper stock and weight: Garda Silk, 100lb text
Printed in Canada by: Friesens Printing

CANADIAN CATALOGUING IN PUBLICATION DATA

Speer, Steve, 1954 –

Building on the Bow, Landmarks in Calgary Commercial Real Estate
ISBN: 978-0-9865753-1-0
First Printing 2012: 1000 hard cover

CONTRIBUTING WRITERS

Foreword by Mayor Naheed Nenshi
Robert Henderson
Michael L. Kehoe, Commercial Real Estate Broker, Fairfield Commercial Real Estate
David Parker
William G.R. Partridge, BOMA Calgary
Richard White, Riddell Kurczaba Architecture Engineering Interior Design Ltd.

CONTRIBUTING EDITORS

Blair Carbert, Stones Carbert Waite LLP
Miles Durrie

Concept development provided by
2011 BOMA Calgary Communications Committee:
Jesse Buhler, Colliers International
Dana Burns, Calgary Herald
Blair Carbert, Stones Carbert Waite LLP
Miles Durrie
Victoria Gibbs, Design Group Staffing Inc.
Roger Hanks, Skyline Roofing Ltd.
Carol Lewis, Calgary Herald
Jay de Nance, Fairfield Commercial Real Estate
Rita Reid, CANMARC a subsidiary of COMINAR REIT

BOMA Calgary is a member driven trade organization dedicated to supporting the commercial real estate industry through advocacy, education and networking. Established in 1969, BOMA is the voice of commercial real estate professionals in Calgary, and its members drive the development of various standards and educational opportunities.

NAHEED K. NENSHI

December 2011

A MESSAGE FROM MAYOR NENSHI

The building where I work, Historic City Hall, was built just over a century ago; we celebrated its 100th birthday on June 26, 2011. In 1911, Calgary was a bustling frontier city and home to approximately 40,000 people. This was before oil and gas changed the course of Calgary's economic future, before the Calgary Stampede, before the Olympics, before just about everything that we know and love about Calgary today.

What is remarkable about Historic City Hall is that it is not the kind of city hall that you build for a city of just 40,000 residents. The sandstone, the clock tower, and the intricate design are representative of a grand vision that Calgarians had for their burgeoning city. The City leadership believed that Calgary was worthy of this beautiful building and that we were to grow into it very soon.

Many of the buildings that you will see throughout this book represent the same foresight that Calgarians had one hundred years ago. They are not necessarily buildings constructed for how things were at the time; they were constructed for the city that the owners wanted and expected to see. These buildings illustrate the dreams we've had for our city.

Calgary has emerged as one of the world's most vibrant and dynamic cities in which to live and work. Over the years, members of BOMA Calgary have adjusted as world events affected Calgary's commercial real estate sector. It is testament to their skill and unwavering optimism in the future of our city that, while most of the world has been pulling back, we are continuing to construct beautiful buildings in anticipation of a very bright future.

I hope that, as you read the essays that accompany the beautiful photographs, you will also imagine how Calgary was at the times these projects were conceived. Two things will soon become clear. The first, and fairly obvious, is that we build beautiful buildings. Second, and perhaps what I am most proud of, is that we are a city that will never settle. We will keep imagining the better Calgary we can have, and then work to turn that into reality.

Sincerely,

Naheed K. Nenshi
MAYOR

Historic City Hall, 700 Macleod Trail South, #8069, Calgary, AB, Canada T2P 2M5
T 403.268.5622 F 403.268.8130 E themayor@calgary.ca

Proudly serving a great city

Artist's Statement

I've been a photographer for over forty years and have always found photography to be an effective tool in slowing the relentless forward pace of life. When I am behind the lens, my sense of time slows down to the point where I am truly *"in the moment"* and this feeling makes me appreciative of photography's ability to put the brakes on life's forward momentum, if even for a moment. My focus is towards fine art photography. The therapeutic nature of exploring urban and rural landscapes with my camera, and seeing with the intensity that photography promotes has been a common thread in my life, something I am extremely grateful for.

I moved to Calgary in 1982 to study photography at the Alberta College of Art. I've always been interested in photographing architecture and derelict buildings, and through my class assignments, or forays on my own, I have been photographing the city consistently since that time. Accessing derelict buildings back in the 80's was simply a matter of walking in, setting up your camera (I almost always use a tripod) and shooting away. Access to the few remaining buildings today is not possible as everything is locked up tight. During my initial meetings with BOMA, we began discussing the buildings we would focus on for the book and I realized how much history I would be covering and the change that has occurred in our city over the years. Buildings such as the Hudson's Bay shed in Inglewood date back to the late 1800's and the Bow, which is under construction as this book is going to print, cover over 100 years of architecture… a pretty daunting task.

The other consideration, for me, was how I would approach the challenge of finding interesting details and make artful imagery from the sixty plus buildings on the shooting list. I knew the book would be monochrome and I would be focusing specifically on exteriors. It would be an exciting challenge to work within these constraints to create images which would be strong enough to draw in a viewer and resonate with their sense of connection. *I hope I have succeeded.*

fourbyfive.com
photography by Steve Speer

Fort Calgary and the CP Railway

From grasslands to urban centre, the Bow River has remained one of the constant features through more than 140 years of exploration, trade and building. According to the Bow River Basin Council, the Bow was originally named Makhabn by the Peigan; the name describes a place where wood for making hunting bows was found. The explorer David Thompson recognized this during his visit circa 1787, and he used the name "Bow River" in his diaries.

In 1871, Fred Kanouse, a partner of the Fort Whoop-Up whisky traders, set up his post—the area's first commercial building—seven miles up the Elbow River from its confluence with the Bow River. From this post, Kanouse traded with the Peigan and Tsuu T'ina people until the arrival of the North-West Mounted Police (NWMP) in 1874.

Four years later, the NWMP contracted the I.G. Baker Company of Fort Benton, Montana Territory, to build a detachment for the police force in what is now Calgary. The structure was completed by mid-December 1875, and I.G. Baker also erected commercial buildings for its own use south of the police post.

At first, the detachment was called The Elbow, then Bow River Fort, then Fort Brisebois. In 1876 NWMP Assistant Commissioner A.G. Irvine recommended to the Justice Minister "Fort Calgary," a suggestion made by the Commissioner, Colonel James Macleod, and the name was adopted by the NWMP. It was named after a region called Calgary Bay on the Isle of Mull, Scotland, which was Macleod's ancestral home. There is debate as to the actual meaning of the word: Place Names of Alberta Vol. II says it is Gaelic for "clear running water" (which Irvine cites in his naming request letter); the City of Calgary website says it means "bay farm"; a professor of Gaelic at Edinburgh University consulted for a 1950 book commemorating Calgary's 75th anniversary claimed the name comes from "Calgaraidh" which, in part, translates to "a place remote"; and the Explore Scotland website says the word derives from "cala ghedarridh," meaning "beach of the meadow."

In 1882-83, Calgary experienced a building boom as Fort Calgary was upgraded from detachment post to District Headquarters. Materials were supplied by Cochrane Ranch Sawmill and the Bow River Mill in Inglewood. Once the new barracks building was completed, the boom waned, as did the influx of newcomers who had driven housing construction.

Land speculators started arriving in late spring 1883, making their best plays for prime land. A factor in this process was the lack of a corporate structure—Calgary had no defined boundaries or government. The land a mile west of Fort Calgary, Section 15, was reserved as grazing land for the NWMP, so the speculators bought up the land east of the Elbow River. The Canadian Pacific Railway crossed the Elbow on August 11, 1883, and set up its first station—a boxcar—a mile west of the fort, off Section 15.

Calgary could now receive train-loads of rail workers, settlers and entrepreneurs, and again a building boom took hold. The CPR had been granted all odd-numbered sections through which its railroad passed, and soon had assigned a survey party to lay out a town plan west of the fort. Section 15 became available in January 1884, the CPR started selling lots, and a civic committee was formed that month with the goal of achieving municipal status for the community.

The community was divided between the CPR town west of the fort and the speculators' town to the east. The deadlock broke when Postmaster James Bannerman moved his flour and feed store, which also served as the area's post office, from east of the Elbow to the new townsite. The land speculators on the east side cut their losses and moved their buildings and businesses near the CPR station. The Town of Calgary, population 506, was incorporated November 7, 1884, by the Territorial Government.

The pace of construction accelerated, and the prime building material was wood. In the fall of 1883, entrepreneurs from Eau Claire, Wisconsin, arrived, secured a timber lease on 100 square miles of the Spray, Bow and Kananaskis rivers. They established the Eau Claire Lumber Company, headquartered in Calgary. A decade later, the Eau Claire and Bow River mills would have sales of more than one million board feet each.

With the completion of the CPR transcontinental railroad on November 7, 1885, work crews were laid off and local suppliers were left with an excess of stock. Another boom had turned to bust, and Calgary now had to rely on a steady stream of incoming settlers to build the community and establish a viable economy based on agriculture.

HUDSON'S BAY SHED, INGLEWOOD
Ninth Avenue and Eighth Street SE

Plate Number 1

EAU CLAIRE & BOW RIVER LUMBER CO.
Eau Claire

Plate Number 2

FORT CALGARY
Ninth Avenue and Seventh Street SE

Plate Number 3

FORT CALGARY
Ninth Avenue and Seventh Street SE

Plate Number 4

EAST END LIVERY AND AUCTION
10th Avenue and 11th Street SE

Plate Number 5

LAST WOOD BUILDING,
TC POWERS & BRO. (PAIN) BLOCK
Stephen Avenue and First Street SW

Plate Number 6

Fire and Sandstone

Calgary burns and rebuilds in sandstone;
introduces new building techniques | 1886–1920

Events took a catastrophic turn when the Parish and Son flour and feed store, on the northwest corner of Atlantic Avenue (now Ninth Avenue) and McTavish Street (now Centre Street), started burning on November 7, 1886. The fire sent embers north and east, sparking a widespread blaze that reduced many businesses in the area to ash. The town, primarily of wood construction, lost 14 buildings and suffered more than $100,000 in damage. A new building boom ensued. Town Council passed a bylaw mandating that fireproof materials be used in rebuilding, triggering a surge of sandstone construction rather than flammable lumber construction. Real estate speculation began to overshadow the agricultural economy. Everyone wanted into the property business, with some downtown lots selling five times in a one-year period.

Calgary became a city in 1894, and saw its population rise to just over 4,000 by the 1901 Dominion Census, and to 43,704 by 1911. By 1905, other building materials were supplanting sandstone, which was considered heavy and Victorian. Brick and terra cotta were seen as lighter, more colourful and reflecting the new age. The Burns Building on Stephen Avenue and First Street S.E. was a brick-core, terra cotta-finished structure completed in 1913. When a traditional look was desired, brick was often used as the load-bearing structure with sandstone as the facing material, as in the case of Calgary's City Hall, (Macleod Trail and Seventh Avenue), officially opened in 1911. One of the last full-curtain-wall sandstone structures built in Calgary was the Grain Exchange Building (Atlantic Avenue, now Ninth Avenue and Scarth Street S.W., now First Street), constructed beginning in 1909.

Its six storeys made it Calgary's first "skyscraper" according to the Calgary Herald. Not only did it reach new heights in elevation, the Grain Exchange was innovative in its use of reinforced concrete, a construction technique that remains standard today. Meanwhile, James Lougheed had come west in the early 1880s to make his fortune, setting up as a lawyer and investing his energies in Calgary's future. He invested, built and, at one time, was paying close to 50 per cent of the city's property taxes. Built between 1899 and 1912, his most prominent buildings comprised the Norman, Clarence, Douglas, Edgar and Lougheed blocks.

Construction of the Lancaster Building on Stephen Avenue and Second Street was started in 1912—shortly before the real estate market collapsed and building again came to a near-standstill. The Lancaster pioneered another new construction technique for Calgary that is still in use. The building has a steel girder core which stood tall as a bare metal skeleton for several years until it could be finished in 1918 with brick and terra cotta. The post office moved in and the Lancaster Building would be the last of Calgary's ornate buildings—and the last major office building erected in Calgary's downtown for the next 35 years.

GRAIN EXCHANGE
Ninth Avenue and First Street SW

Plate Number 7

LANCASTER BUILDING
Stephen Avenue and Second Street SW

Plate Number 8

ALBERTA HOTEL
Stephen Avenue and First Street SW

Plate Number 9

DOLL BLOCK
Stephen Avenue and First Street SE

Plate Number 10

KING EDWARD HOTEL
Ninth Avenue and Fourth Street SE

Plate Number 11

CALGARY CITY HALL
Stephen Avenue and Macleod Trail SE

Plate Number 12

IMPERIAL BANK, LINEHAM BLOCK
Stephen Avenue and Centre Street SE

Plate Number 13

DOMINION BANK
Stephen Avenue and First Street SE

Plate Number 14

MACPHERSON FRUIT CO.
Stephen Avenue and Second Street SW

Plate Number 15

CALGARY HERALD BLOCK
Stephen Avenue and First Street SW

Plate Number 16

HOLLINGSWORTH BUILDING, BANKERS HALL
Stephen Avenue and Second Street SW

Plate Number 17

LOUGHEED BUILDING
Sixth Avenue and First Street SW

Plate Number 18

FAIRMONT PALLISER HOTEL
Ninth Avenue and First Street SW

Plate Number 19

CANADIAN BANK OF COMMERCE
12th Avenue and First Street SW

Plate Number 20

ODD FELLOWS TEMPLE
Sixth Avenue and Centre Street SW

Plate Number 21

SIMMONS BUILDING

Confluence Way and Fifth Street SE

Plate Number 22

BURNS BUILDING
Stephen Avenue and Macleod Trail SE

Plate Number 23

HUDSON'S BAY COMPANY
Stephen Avenue and First Street SW

Plate Number 24

The War Years

Real estate collapses as the war effort takes hold;
land and office space become plentiful | **1920–1950**

The collapse of the real estate market and associated construction industry resulted in considerable unemployment. For four years, 1914-18, Calgary was part of the First World War effort. When the war ended in late 1918, Calgary was a far different place from the boomtown of five years earlier. The commercial office building spree was finished. Calgary had more office space than businesses to fill it, and through the 1920s the City acquired many properties by tax forfeiture.

A small flurry of pre-Great Depression activity in 1928-29 saw some commercial development. Alexander Corner on Scarth Street and Stephen Avenue succumbed to expansion when the Hudson's Bay Company store crossed the lane and established a presence on Stephen Avenue. The Bank of Montreal on Scarth Street replaced its old turreted main branch across the street, and the T. Eaton Company opened its new department store between Barclay Street (now Third Street S.W.) and Ross Street (now Fourth Street) on Stephen Avenue. Limestone was a popular material, used for both these buildings.

The York Hotel, on Seventh Avenue, constructed through the winter of 1929-30 and opened in April, stood out as the first continuous-pour concrete structure in Calgary. Otherwise, construction lagged during the Depression. Commercial office space still remained plentiful, rents were low and the stock market crash had terminated any building prospects. Depression-era work relief projects included using teams of unemployed workers to remove the streetcar tracks that had been laid in 1909.

The City had acquired considerable land over the previous 20 years at an expense, and that land did not contribute to the tax coffers. Beginning in 1941, city council began to dispose of land assessed at $5 million for 50 per cent, and later 25 per cent, of assessed value. In 1910, house lots in Hillhurst sold for up to $1,200 each. In 1941, the Mayland Heights subdivision was sold for $25 an acre and some building lots were sold for $25 each.

Calgary still boasted plenty of office buildings and space was easily had. While Calgary had become an industry management centre since the opening of the Turner Valley oilfields beginning in 1914, the Second World War finally triggered significant demand for oil. The war effort increased the use of the internal combustion engine, and petroleum production demands increased. Output at Turner Valley peaked at 9.7 million barrels in 1942, but then declined. Calgary needed a new oil find to boost the industry, fire up the economy, and break the slow growth of the city.

BANK OF MONTREAL
Stephen Avenue and First Street SW

Plate Number 25

W.A. GOUGH, VIOLIN SERVICE
16th Avenue and Centre Street NW

Plate Number 26

THE BANK OF NOVA SCOTIA
Stephen Avenue and First Street SW

Plate Number 27

CALGARY PUBLIC BUILDING
Stephen Avenue and Macleod Trail SE

Plate Number 28

Oil Boom

The 1950s were transformational as the city moved from early 20th century sandstone commercial structures to modern office buildings, shopping centres and industrial parks. Imperial Oil found a major source of oil at Leduc in 1947 and Calgary quickly moved beyond regional branch office status into a major corporate centre for the oil and gas industry in Canada, as well as the commercial hub of Southern Alberta. Commercial real estate development saw a spike in growth accompanied by unprecedented population increases and economic prosperity. Every aspect of real estate was in a growth phase as homebuilders created vast residential subdivisions. The first industrial parks were opened and the demand for office and retail space exploded.

New suburbs at the outskirts of the city accelerated the transition from the traditional downtown shopping experience to suburban plazas and, eventually, to regional shopping centres. Post-war suburban consumerism in Calgary and the development of new roadways led to record residential construction, and retail followed. In 1953, the Britannia neighbourhood shopping centre was the first purpose-built shopping centre in Calgary, and became the template for other suburban strip plazas that soon followed across the city. Forest Lawn, Bowness and Montgomery were separate satellite communities at the time, and each featured its own retail strip. By 1958, department store Simpsons-Sears (now Sears Canada) opened at the North Hill Shopping Centre, the city's first regional shopping centre.

In the spring of 1951, the Barron Building opened on Eighth Avenue as Calgary's first mixed-use commercial building. Some publicity at the time claimed it was the city's first skyscraper, although the 41-year-old Grain Exchange Building had also claimed this distinction. This landmark project was significant in the city's commercial real estate history; the Barron Building combined retail, office space and the Uptown Theatre. It became home to Sun Oil, Shell, Socony-Vacuum Oil, Mobil Oil and TransCanada Pipelines. By 1955, head offices and branch offices of Canadian and American oil and gas firms were flooding into Calgary, along with the geologists, geophysical firms, land agents, lawyers and oil brokers fuelling the office space boom. In June 1958, the City of Calgary zoning bylaw was amended to increase the height and density of office buildings from 12 to 20 storeys with a maximum eight times the site coverage. Other significant office buildings soon followed, including the Royalite Building on Seventh Avenue S.W. in 1955 and the Petro-Chemical Building on Eighth Avenue in 1958.

The City of Calgary created the first planned, dedicated industrial area in 1954; the Manchester district in southeast Calgary accommodated an influx of oil-well drilling, oilfield service, construction and pipeline firms moving to the city. By 1958, other new industrial and warehousing districts, such as Highfield, Bonnybrook and Meridian, further solidified Calgary as a regional distribution and service hub.

THE BARRON BUILDING
Eighth Avenue and Fifth Street SW

Plate Number 29

NORTH HILL SHOPPING CENTRE
16th Avenue and 14th Street NW

Plate Number 30

BRITANNIA BUILDING
Sixth Avenue and Sixth Street SW

Plate Number 31

Pushing the Limits

Although Calgary was enjoying a healthy increase in new residents as it headed into the 1960s, it was still a small city, with a population of about 235,000.

Only a couple of big buildings dominated the downtown area. The importance of the surrounding farm community was shown in a huge structure further west along Ninth Avenue—Robin Hood Flour Mills Ltd., which stood where Gulf Canada Square sits today until 1973.

The city's core would become home to the first skyscraper complex. Calgarians showed a lot of interest by peeping through viewing holes to catch a glimpse of the $5-million, 20-storey Elveden House (another claimant to the title of first skyscraper in Calgary) rise out of a huge hole on Seventh Avenue S.W. in 1960. By the middle of the decade they had also watched as the British American Oil Company and Guinness House were also completed on the site.

Calgarians saw the continuous pour of concrete that rose up 626 feet (191 metres) to become the Husky Tower (now Calgary Tower). Built as a joint venture between Husky Oil and Marathon Realty, in part to mark Canada's Centennial, it was labelled as the tallest structure west of Toronto when it was completed in 1968. The land on either side was soon developed as Palliser Square with retail stores and an office tower.

The pace of downtown construction quickened considerably in the 1970s when oil reached the then-staggering price of $11 per barrel. Among the most significant projects were Shell Centre and the blocks along Stephen Avenue Mall between Eaton's and The Bay. This block would eventually become home to TD Square (originally Oxford Square), the Dome Petroleum, Home Oil and Scotia Centre towers, and the publicly acclaimed Devonian Gardens, an indoor garden in TD Square, opened in 1977.

The Royal Bank Building on Second Street and the Stock Exchange Tower on Fifth Avenue helped point to the city's growing financial power, and the four-tower Bow Valley Square took up a complete city block. The Calgary Inn (now the Westin) was built as a first-class hotel, and the Harry Hays Building was completed on a prime location along the Bow River to house federal government offices.

Outside of the downtown core, Calgary also saw increasing suburban growth. The North Hill Shopping Centre, anchored on its east end by Simpsons-Sears, was the largest facility of its kind in Western Canada when it opened in 1958; originally an outdoor strip mall, it was expanded and enclosed in 1973. Its early competition included Brentwood Mall (later called Brentwood Village Mall), which opened in 1961 as an open-air mall, and was enclosed in 1970 (only to later partially revert to an open-air mall in the 2000s).

But the biggest addition to Calgary's suburban shopping scene came when Chinook Shopping Centre opened in August of 1960 on the site of the former Chinook Drive-In Theatre, boasting 45 stores—including anchor tenant Woodward's department and grocery store, and a bowling alley—covering more than 481,000 square feet.

In 1965, Chinook underwent a renovation that added an office tower and enclosed the mall. That same year, Southridge Mall opened across the street from Chinook Shopping Centre, with an 80,000-square-foot Simpsons-Sears store and a Loblaws grocery store. Although they were two separate entities, shoppers began to think of them as one. The two malls ultimately were physically merged in 1974; since 1971 they had been known as Chinook-Ridge Centre, but with the merger the facility became simply Chinook Centre. Not to be outdone, another large shopping centre, Market Mall, opened in the fast-growing northwest in 1971 while, to serve the growing south end of the city, Southcentre mall opened in 1974.

Those who arrived by aircraft to join Calgary's growing population in the early 1960s probably taxied up to the airport and descended steps onto the tarmac and into the terminal then located on Aviation Boulevard. About 1966, the former McCall Field was rechristened Calgary International Airport and, in 1977, a new terminal was officially opened.

CHINOOK CENTRE
Macleod Trail and Glenmore Trail SW

Plate Number 32

TD SQUARE
Seventh Avenue and Second Street SW

Plate Number 33

SCOTIA CENTRE
Stephen Avenue and Second Street SW

Plate Number 34

MOUNT ROYAL VILLAGE
16th Avenue and Eighth Street SW

Plate Number 35

CALGARY HERALD BUILDING
Seventh Avenue and First Street SW

Plate Number 36

PALLISER SQUARE
Ninth Avenue and Centre Street SE

Plate Number 37

ELVEDEN CENTRE
Seventh Avenue and Sixth Street SW

Plate Number 38

MARKET MALL

32nd Avenue and Shaganappi Trail NW

Plate Number 39

SOUTHLAND PARK 4
Macleod Trail and Southland Drive SW

Plate Number 40

CALGARY INTERNATIONAL AIRPORT
Airport Road NE

Plate Number 41

SOUTHCENTRE EXECUTIVE TOWER
Willow Park Drive and Macleod Trail SE

Plate Number 42

GULF CANADA SQUARE
Ninth Avenue and Third Street SW

Plate Number 43

BOW VALLEY SQUARE
Sixth Avenue and First Street SW

Plate Number 44

Crisis and Recovery

Impact of the NEP on commercial real estate
and its positive recovery | **1980–2000**

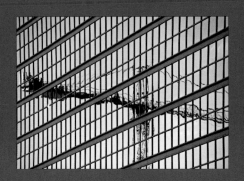

The oil business continued to drive the economy, but the 1980s brought diversification as Calgary took on the role of financial centre with the increased presence of all the major banks. Third Street S.W. (Barclay Mall) became Calgary's equivalent of Wall Street because of the dominance of financial institutions nearby. Bank of Montreal's First Canadian Centre, Scotia Centre and the Royal Bank Building, as well as the Alberta Stock Exchange Tower. More than 50 buildings were built or started during this time, though some were never completed. One of the most significant was the two-tower Petro-Canada Centre (now Suncor Energy Centre), completed in 1984. When finished, the West Tower, the taller of the two, was the highest building in Canada outside of Toronto (reclaiming a title once held by the Husky/Calgary Tower); because of the sloping shape of the buildings' tops, the exact number of storeys in the West Tower is a matter of debate, with 52 cited by the building's owner, and others citing numbers from 52 to 56.

Economic disaster struck for Calgary in 1980 when federal government, as part of its budget, introduced the National Energy Program (NEP). NEP policies, which included revenue sharing with Ottawa, coincided with a downturn in the price of oil and together those sparked a bust in the Calgary economy. Almost immediately, commercial construction came to a halt. By 1986 the policy was eliminated, but the NEP's aftereffects continued. Construction of the east tower of Bankers Hall by Trizec at Stephen Avenue and Second Street, completed in 1989, signified the end of the downturn and the beginning of the next era of the city's commercial evolution.

There was also growing interest in areas outside of the downtown core. The population had increased by about 50 per cent between 1971 and 1981 from approximately 400,000 to 600,000. The city's Beltline district grew with the phase two addition of the Mount Royal Village mixed-use project on the corner of Eighth Street and 16th Avenue S.W.

The deep south of the city also saw development with the addition of the Southland Park office complex, adjacent to a new light rail transit (LRT) station; construction of the complex began in 1978 and its fourth building was added in 2008.

Calgary hosted the Olympic Winter Games in 1988. New and interesting structures appeared in the years leading up to the games, including the Olympic Saddledome (1983) and Olympic Oval (1987), while the Stampede Park's Big Four Building (1959) underwent renovations in order to host the international broadcast centre for the games. The ski jump tower at the brand-new Canada Olympic Park marked the city's western horizon.

Additional major buildings constructed in this period include the Canterra Tower (now Devon Tower) in 1988, the Ernst & Young Tower in 2000, the west tower of Bankers Hall in 2000, and the expansion of the Calgary (now Telus) Convention centre in 2000.

BANKERS HALL
Stephen Avenue and Second Street SW

Plate Number 45

EATON CENTRE
Stephen Avenue and Third Street SW

Plate Number 46

FIFTH AVENUE PLACE
Fifth Avenue and Second Street SW

Plate Number 47

FIRST CANADIAN CENTRE
Seventh Avenue and Third Street SW

Plate Number 48

CALGARY TELUS CONVENTION CENTRE
Stephen Avenue and First Street SE

Plate Number 49

PETRO-CANADA CENTRE
Fifth Avenue and Centre Street SW

Plate Number 50

SHAW COURT
Third Avenue and Sixth Street SW

Plate Number 51

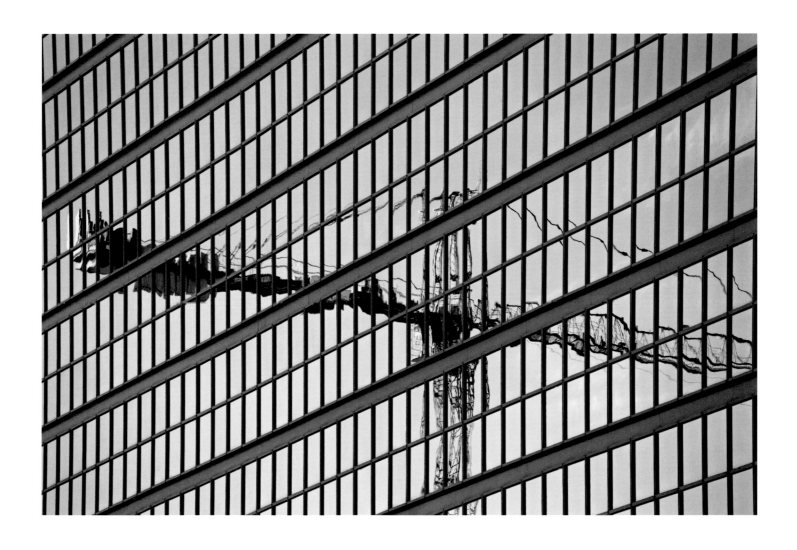

CALGARY MUNICIPAL BUILDING
Stephen Avenue and Macleod Trail SE

Plate Number 52

WESTERN CANADIAN PLACE
Ninth Avenue and Sixth Street SW

Plate Number 53

Dense and Diverse

Investing in commercial space and expanding
beyond city boundaries | 2000–2012

During the first decade of the 21st century, the pace of change in Calgary accelerated. Density increased throughout most of its business and industrial zones. The population crossed the one million threshold in 2006. While still largely reliant on the oil and gas sector, the economic base diversified as the logistics industry emerged and Calgary's role as a product-distribution hub grew. The city also continued to hold its well-established place as a location of choice for head offices. By 2008, the Calgary International Airport was moving 12.5 million passengers annually and major construction plans were announced that would double the size of the airport, adding a second north-south runway by 2015.

Major national development groups were investing heavily in Calgary and its future, and with good reason. A massive Shaw Communications building in the northeast (2005), Centennial Place (2010), Jamieson Place (2010), and downtown's most recent signature building, The Bow which started construction in 2007 and is expected to be completed in 2012, were all built in this period. Some older architecture disappeared as the old Penny Lane shopping centre, which was created in 1973 from historic buildings dating back to the turn of the 20th century, was demolished in 2007, and replaced by Eighth Avenue Place in 2011.

Calgary was now a major metropolitan centre and building was not restricted to the City's corporate limits. CrossIron Mills, a huge retail complex built just north of the city, opened in 2009 as the first new enclosed shopping mall in the Calgary area in a generation, representing a shift in focus away from the more conventional shopping outlets, and from the big-box power centres that emerged in the 1990s. Beginning in the late 1990s, most major retail centres in Calgary were expanded, renovated and modernized, including Chinook Centre, North Hill Shopping Centre, Market Mall, Southcentre, Sunridge Mall, and, in 2011, the former TD Square and Eaton Centre malls completed a renovation and merger to become The Core.

DEVON TOWER
Third Avenue and Third Street SW

Plate Number 54

CENTENNIAL PLACE
Third Avenue and Fourth Street SW

Plate Number 55

HOTEL LE GERMAIN
Ninth Avenue and Centre Street SW

Plate Number 56

JAMIESON PLACE
Fourth Avenue and Second Street SW

Plate Number 57

CENTRIUM PLACE
Sixth Avenue and Third Street SW

Plate Number 58

CROSSIRON MILLS
CrossIron Boulevard, Rocky View

Plate Number 59

LIVINGSTON PLACE
Third Avenue and Second Street SW

Plate Number 60

IBM CAMPUS
11th Avenue and Second Street SW

Plate Number 61

EIGHTH AVENUE PLACE
Ninth Avenue and Fifth Street SW

Plate Number 62

THE BOW
Sixth Avenue and Centre Street SE

Plate Number 63

Building on the Bow

Imagining what will be for the city built on the Bow River | **The Future**

What will the future bring? As Calgary celebrates the 100th anniversaries of the Calgary Stampede, the Calgary Public Library and the City of Calgary Recreation Department in 2012, the city is also grappling with new challenges and opportunities. Politicians and developers, in collaboration with the public, need to embrace the new realities if Calgary is to evolve into one of the world's premier cities.

The Simmons Building is a landmark of the commercial real estate past, and 100 years after its construction, it is the symbol of the new East Village community. With the East Village changing the landscape of the urban core, Calgary may continue to be a downtown-focused city. Or the city could decentralize, evolving into a collection of smaller hubs each with its own economic engine. Think of Calgary's northwest, with the University of Calgary, SAIT Polytechnic and Foothills Medical Centre campuses fostering medicine, science and technology; the far southeast with its new South Health Campus, set to open in 2012; and the northeast with its concentration of transportation, warehousing and logistics facilities around the Calgary International Airport. Each of these could become increasingly self-contained, with further residential development in each to support the need for workers, and retail to serve those populations.

Downtown could get its first 100-plus-floor office tower— or perhaps the skyscraper will become the dinosaur of the 21st century. Office skyscrapers may emerge in the suburbs, if downtown's monopoly as home for the major oil and gas corporate headquarters comes to an end. As green design permeates architecture, office towers may begin to incorporate wind turbines and solar panels as part of their design, making them energy self-sufficient. If that is the case, perhaps old office towers will become the 21st century's version of the 20th century's loft warehouse condo.

Perhaps mixed-use development will become the norm, rather than single-use communities. Segregated land-use zoning could become a thing of the past, along with suburban power centres and big-box developments, as they are replaced by "High Street" retail with residential and offices above. There will likely be mega-makeovers of the Shawnessy, Signal Hill/ Westhills, Beacon Hill, Crowfoot and Country Hills power centres, as well as the transformation of Deerfoot, Sunridge and Marlborough malls into new town centres.

Calgarians will be asked to embrace a more diverse and dense city. Transit-oriented developments at LRT stations (such as the one planned at the new station by Westbrook Mall) and along major road corridors will be the norm. It seems a possibility that the ring road, the southeast extension of the LRT line and a high-speed rail link to Edmonton will all be completed over the next 50 years. These megaprojects will reshape the city radically.

In the 20th century, Calgary evolved from a city of pioneers to a city of sandstone, and later to one of skyscrapers and suburbs. In the 21st century, Calgary's developers, architects, engineers and planners will continue to adopt, adapt and create new commercial building technologies and designs, and new planning visions, as dictated by a sophisticated and dynamic economic and social reality.

This publication was made possible through the generous support of the following:

ALLIED PROPERTIES
REAL ESTATE INVESTMENT TRUST

AVISON YOUNG

Intelligent
Real Estate Solutions

Bentall
Kennedy

Cadillac
Fairview

DUNDEE

R E I T

Hines

Ivanhoé
Cambridge

Caisse de dépôt et placement
du Québec

LABBE-LEECH
INTERIORS LTD.

QUALICO®

OXFORD

SKYLINE
Roofing Ltd.

Servpro®
CLEANING

photography by Steve Speer